10-2-20
$ 23.95

RENOIR

THE GREAT ARTISTS COLLECTION

MASON CREST

Contents

2

*Great Works order is alphabetical where possible.

RENOIR

Mason Crest
450 Parkway Drive, Suite D
Broomall, PA 19008
www.masoncrest.com

©2016 by Mason Crest, an imprint of National Highlights, Inc.

Printed and bound in the United States of America.

10 9 8 7 6 5 4 3 2

Cataloging-in-Publication Data on file with the Library of Congress.

Series ISBN: 978-1-4222-3256-9
Hardback ISBN: 978-1-4222-3262-0
ebook ISBN: 978-1-4222-8539-8

Written by: Sabine Miller

Images courtesy of PA Photos and Scala Archives

"An artist, under pain of oblivion, must have confidence in himself, and listen only to his real master: Nature."
Pierre-Auguste Renoir

Introduction

(Public Domain)

■ **ABOVE: Pierre-Auguste Renoir.**

Renoir was renowned for his works, with their vibrant light and color and the harmony of the lines he portrayed within his landscapes and figure paintings. At the beginning of his prolific career he employed the Impressionist techniques, where detail was denied and replaced with soft fusions between characters and their surroundings. While he moved away from this style in the middle of his career – known as his Ingres Period, where he concentrated on more definition like the conventional and traditional painters – he returned to the softness of his earlier style toward the end of his life.

Renoir was greatly influenced by artists such as Rubens, Titian, Raphael, Eugène Delacroix, and his contemporary and friend, Claude Monet (1840-1926). He was also interested in the works of Gustave Courbet, Édouard Manet, and Camille Carot and their influence is also clearly seen in a number of Renoir's works. Alongside Monet, he became obsessed with painting en plein air (in the open air) and exploring the subject matter provided by the open countryside toward the late 1860s. He firmly believed that black did not produce a shadow, but that shadows were reflected color of the objects surrounding them. He was ready to be influenced by the Impressionist movement, which didn't even have a name when he started out on his experimental journey.

Impressionism was a 19th-century art movement that began with a number of Paris-based artists who were disillusioned with the official Paris Salon. It was Monet's *Impression, Sunrise,* described in a derogatory comment by art critic Louis Leroy as an "impression," which gave the movement its name. While the critic had hoped to ridicule Monet and his fellow artists in a satiric review in *Le Charivari,* about the first Impression exhibition in 1874, they liked the name he applied, and the term stuck. In Impressionism, the brushstrokes are visible and the open compositions looked unfinished to the art elite in Paris. The changing qualities of the effect of light were of paramount importance to the new movement, and it became usual to accentuate the effects of the passage of time over subject. It was all about the visual aspect of the paintings and the experience for the audience along with the effect that light had on the senses.

Many new movements usually began in literature; however, Impressionism first became initiated before transferring to other forms of media, including music and literature. The Impressionists were considered a

(Mary Evans/Epic/Tallandier)

■ ABOVE: Gustave Courbet (1819-1877), in his workshop studio with a palette.

(Mary Evans Picture Library)

■ **ABOVE:** Édouard Manet (1832-1883), a great French impressionist painter, c. 1875.

highly radical movement who "broke the rules" of academic painting. Colors began to take prominence and brushstrokes became fragmented – broken – and working in the studio became a thing of the past. Outside – en plein air – was considered the most favored way to paint. Up to this point, even landscapes had been painted in the studio, but the Impressionists found that by working outdoors they could capture the realistic scenes of modern-day life while emphasizing the vivid effects of light on the subject. Details were overlooked, as was the previous blending of colors that had been so carefully mixed by generations of artists before. Now, colors were

used unmixed to provide an intense richness never seen before. New techniques were developed that became synonymous with Impressionism. Movement became a particularly "real" element in the style. Ripples of water, flowing rivers, and choppy seas were all brought to life through the use of fragmented brushstrokes, while the sunlight highlighted and illuminated the effect. It was a breathtaking and daring move. Radical and revolutionary. The poses and compositions were candid, were unafraid of immediacy, and created movement. To begin with, critics, and the public alike, were shocked by the works of the Impressionists. Their paintings – which provided

■ **ABOVE:** Claude Monet, who was a close friend and contemporary of Renoir, photographed at work in 1923.

emotion and intimacy – were little understood by audiences of the day. Their reaction was quite hostile to start, although gradually they began to recognize that the Impressionists had created an original vision. It was fresh, full of vitality, and offered a "breath of fresh air," a freedom that captured the essence of everyday events and subject matter. This would eventually lead to sensations becoming important in other movements including Post-Impressionism, Fauvism, and Cubism.

Impressionism grew in the wake of the redevelopment of Paris as directed by Emperor Napoleon III, who commissioned Baron Haussmann to change the landscape of the city to one of large open boulevards and sweeping vistas as opposed to the former tiny, overcrowded streets. The Académie des Beaux-Arts

dominated the French art scene in the 19th century and was traditional in its approach to historical, mythical, and religious themes. The middle of the century saw portraits valued while landscapes and still life were considered in poor taste. Color was conservative at best and brushstrokes were invisible. The Académie favored carefully composed works of reality. Emotions were concealed and paintings were devoid of personality. The work of the Impressionists, which went against all that the Académie held dear, was clearly mind blowing at the time. Quite simply, their work was considered unacceptable. The official Paris Salon – the annual art show – enabled artists to enhance their standing in the art world, to build their reputations, gain commissions, and win prizes. The work of the Impressionists was

(Mary Evans Picture Library/Imagno)

■ **ABOVE:** *Impression, Sunrise*, 1872, by Monet, was painted in Le Havre, France. Critics called Monet and his circle – at first ironically – "Impressionists" after the title of this work.

systematically refused acceptance by the Salon.

The Salon of the Refused (Salon des Refusés) was created with the permission of Napoleon who decreed that the public should judge the works for themselves. Many of the public did not understand the art of the Salon des Refusés – many openly laughed at the presented paintings – but, from 1863 onward, Impressionism was to surge forward. Further Salons were refused and the young artists decided to fight back by opening their own exhibition. Renoir, Monet, Pissarro, Sisley, Morisot, and Degas among others, organized a show at the studio of Nadar, a renowned photographer. Progressive artists were invited to exhibit, including Boudin. It was to be the first Impressionist exhibition of eight (held between 1874 and 1886).

Renoir was never considered a pure Impressionist – but the spirit of independence and its revolutionary approach bound him to the group. He turned from the movement for a time, defecting in the 1880s. He turned his attentions to the official Salon once again. A great supporter of his work (and those of other young aspiring artists) was the art dealer Paul Durand-Ruel who kept the movement alive by organizing shows across the globe, notably in New York and London. He bought many works himself and Renoir was rewarded with success at the Paris Salon in 1879. By the 1890s, forms of Impressionism had become accepted by the Salon.

Color and light greatly reflected the style of Impressionism. Brushstrokes were short, fast, and thick capturing the essence of the subject or theme. Colors were applied side by side – it was for the audience to blend them on visual impact – and wet paint was applied to wet paint to provide softer edges and a mix of colors. Impressionists also preferred not to use glazes, employed by earlier artists to build up effects. Natural light was a carefully crafted technique developed by the movement – where close attention was paid to the reflection of colors.

What the movement achieved was fresh, free, and bold. Renoir developed his own techniques based on the style. Paints were now available in tubes, premixed, and Renoir took advantage of their availability to create his own masterpieces. He became a renowned commentator on modern-day life in France and was expressive in his approach. His works are gentle, tranquil, and serene in nature and provide audiences with a snapshot of the past from the later part of the 19th century and into the early 20th century. The development of photography – once thought of as a possible rival to the world of art – positively encouraged artists of the late 19th century. Artists actively sought to find different means of artistic expression, and this came in the form of expressing perceptions of nature. Depictions became subjective and color became the medium of choice – at a time when photography was only available in black and white. Unconventional compositions on Japanese art prints and wood also played a part in artistic developments of the time.

Renoir celebrated beauty in all its forms. He was particularly interested in female sensuality and many of his paintings were of nudes. He was a prolific artist of figures and turned away from landscapes in order to capture the essence of figures and often used his friends and family in his works. In fact, when it came to large groups of figures, he would paint in his friends and associates so that his works became large versions of portraitures rather than just a crowd scene. While being a founding member of the Impressionist movement, Renoir is perhaps known for his depictions of pretty children, flowers, idyllic scenes, and his nudes; *The Bathers* and *Nude in the Sun* are perhaps amongst his most sensual works. He was devoted to his painting throughout his life and experimented right up to his death in 1919. He was passionate about his work and, when crippled with arthritis toward the end, would have his paintbrushes strapped to his right hand (although many commentators cite that the bandages were there

■ **RIGHT:** *The Seine at Champrosay* or *The Banks of the Seine at Champrosay*, **1876, by Renoir.**

to avoid skin irritation and that he could actually still hold the brushes himself), so that he could continue with the enduring love he had for his masterpieces.

Renoir's paintings are often described as being easily recognizable for their use of bright colors and bold lines. He developed a sunny, joyful, outlook in his works and spent his early years sketching on the banks of the Seine, alongside Monet. It was this time of experimentation with Monet that led to the use of bright colors that became so central to the Impressionist movement. He didn't consider his works moralistic or political and he often represented non-serious themes. He had a complete mastery of facial features, making his portraiture commissions engaging and particularly lifelike. He loved to paint women and he was always sympathetic and generous in his depictions of women. One of the other areas in which he excelled was the "movement" he created within his pieces, particularly when painting water – the fast, fragmented brushstrokes with the light effects of the sun beaming down and the shadows created by the subjects he painted are simply breathtaking and unique. It is cited that Renoir only ever used five colors on his palette because his time as a highly revered porcelain painter at the very beginning

■ **ABOVE:** Exhibitions of art took place at the Salon de Paris on an annual basis; this illustration is c. 1868.

■ **BELOW:** A caricature of photographer Nadar. The Impressionist artists held their first exhibition at his studio.

■ **ABOVE:** *Nude in the Sun*, 1875-1876, by Renoir. Musee d'Orsay, Paris.

14

of his career had taught him how to combine colors to great effect.

In his later years, Renoir returned to the thin brushstrokes he had used earlier in his career. He became less concerned with outlines and created softer pieces that had a sketchy approach. His style changed at the end of his career to once again include stronger colors – including reds and oranges applied with thick brushstrokes. It was at this time that the nude featured as the dominant subject of his paintings.

(Mary Evans/Epic/Tallandier)

■ **ABOVE:** Paul Durand-Ruel, the French art dealer who helped keep the Impressionist movement alive.

■ **LEFT:** Renoir working in his studio in Cagnes-sur-Mer, France, c. 1915.

Renoir
A Biography

(Mary Evans/Epic/Tallandier)

■ **ABOVE:** A youthful Pierre-Auguste Renoir in a drawing by Marcellin Desboutin.

Pierre-Auguste Renoir was born in Limoges, Haute-Vienne, France on February 25, 1841. Born to a working-class family, he worked in a porcelain factory as a young boy where his drawing talents led to his being chosen to paint designs on fine china. He was just 13 years old. Prior to enrolling at an art school, he decorated fans and painted hangings for missionaries. It was during this time that he visited the Louvre in Paris to study the works of the old masters. In 1862, at the age of 21, he began studying with Charles Gleyre in France's capital city where he met

(PA Photos)

■ **ABOVE:** Renoir gave some of his pictures to Queen Victoria on the occasion of her Golden Jubilee, 1887.

Claude Monet, Alfred Sisley, and Frédéric Bazille. Like many of his contemporaries – particularly Monet – Renoir suffered severe financial difficulties and could often not afford the paints he needed for his studies. He persevered and was eventually accepted by the Paris Salon in 1864. It would be another 10 years, however, before recognition for his works would be fully realized. One of the main reasons for this was the Franco-Prussian War, which resulted in Bazille's untimely death in 1870 and Monet's escape to London in the UK. In 1871, Renoir was accused of being a spy as he sat painting on the banks of the Seine. The

group of Communards was about to throw him into the river when, luckily, he was recognized by Raoul Rigault, whom he had protected in an earlier affray during the difficult climate. Although he had thrived painting en plein air for a number of years, his decade-long association with fellow artist Jules Le Coeur came to an end, and his favorite location for working just outside Fontainebleau was denied. It led to a change in the direction of his works.

Having become disillusioned with the conventional Salon, Renoir, alongside his peers, chose to work in the newly developing Impressionist style. He showed six

(Mary Evans/Iberfoto)

■ **ABOVE:** A polychrome plaster sculpture by Renoir of Aline Charigot, who married him in 1890.

(PA Photos)

■ **ABOVE:** Renoir had three sons; pictured here is Jean Renoir who became a renowned movie director.

■ **RIGHT:** French director Jean Renoir (second from left) and his brother Claude, called Coco, seated on the ground.

■ **BELOW:** Gabrielle Renard looked after the Renoir children.

(Mary Evans/Epic/Tallandier)

(Mary Evans/Epic/Tallandier)

paintings in the first Impressionist exhibition in 1874, (the same year that Paul Durand-Ruel showed two of his works in London), but his interest in the movement was on the decline over successive years. Renoir was a keen traveler and set off for Algeria in 1881 before moving on to Madrid where he studied the works of Diego Velázquez. He then traveled to Italy where he viewed the masterpieces of Titian and Raphael. It was at this time (in 1882) that he met the German composer, Wagner, whom he greatly admired. However, he was back in Algeria later that same

year having contracted pneumonia. He was desperately ill and spent six weeks recovering in the warmer climes – his respiratory system was permanently damaged. He spent just over a month in Guernsey in the Channel Islands from September the following year where he painted around 15 highly revered pieces.

Renoir spent the next years back in Paris where he lived and worked in the popular Montmartre. Here he met Suzanne Valadon, who he employed as a model. She posed for *The Bathers*. When Queen Victoria celebrated

her Golden Jubilee in 1887, Renoir was asked to submit a number of works to a catalog of French Impressionist paintings – he provided them as a gesture of his loyalty.

Renoir married his long-time companion, lover, and muse, Aline Victorine Charigot, in 1890. The couple's first son, Pierre, was born five years earlier in 1885 on March 21. (Pierre Renoir became a noted actor on both stage and in movies. He died in Paris at the age of 66 on March 11, 1952.) It is cited that Renoir took wholeheartedly to fatherhood. He was interested in his children and took

(Public Domain)

■ **ABOVE:** The old village of Haut-de-Cagnes (Cagnes-sur-Mer) to where Renoir and his family moved to help with his rheumatoid arthritis.

great pride in bringing them up – two more sons were born to the couple in later years. Following the marriage, Renoir was keen to paint everyday family life. When the couple's second son, Jean, was born in September 1894, the young Gabrielle Renard, cousin of Aline, joined the household in order to help with looking after the children and the house. Gabrielle became a regular model for

Renoir whom it is said she adored. (Jean Renoir became a celebrated moviemaker and director in the United States. He died in Beverly Hills at the age of 84 on February 12, 1979.) Claude Renoir was the couple's third child, born in 1901. (He was also a moviemaker and died in 1969.)

By the time of Jean's birth, Renoir had been suffering from rheumatoid arthritis for about two years. As a result,

(Mary Evans/Sueddeutsche Zeitung Photo)

■ **ABOVE:** Renoir pictured during his later years.

the family moved in 1907 to Cagnes-sur-Mer with its Mediterranean climate. Renoir was suffering greatly from his arthritis and became wheelchair bound. As a result of the crippling affliction he developed severe deformities in his hands and ankylosis in his right shoulder. It led to another change in painting technique, while he also developed a sculpting style, aided by Richard Guino, who worked the clay for him. Aline was the love of Renoir's life and was immortalized in many of his paintings. She was 23 years younger than her husband but died four years before him on June 27, 1915. She was buried in the churchyard at Essoyes, where the family lived when they were not resident in Paris or Cagnes-sur-Mer. When Renoir died on December 3, 1919, he was buried alongside his wife.

Great Works

Paintings

A Girl with a Watering Can
(1876)

- Oil on canvas, 39.4 in x 28.7 in (100 cm x 73 cm)

Renoir, Pierre Auguste (1841-1919): Girl with watering can, 1876. Washington DC, National Gallery of Art. © 2013. DeAgostini Picture Library/Scala, Florence

This painting has been much admired and revered by generations, and it's highly likely that this is what Renoir was hoping for. The first Impressionist exhibition in 1874 brought Renoir and his contemporaries a fair amount of notoriety – rather than money – and Renoir struggled financially to both fund his painting and make money from his art. He organized an auction of his works in 1875, which proved a financial disaster. His poor, working-class background did not afford him the means by which to survive easily and he found himself in a constant struggle in his earlier career. It is suggested that by painting a small, pretty child he would draw attention to his potential and hope to land himself a wealthy patron or a number of portraiture commissions. Impressionism was concerned with quick brushstrokes, light effects on the subject, and nature. While being an important exponent of Impressionism, Renoir was always led back to painting figures. The blues, greens, and bright colors of this piece show how, rather than blending his colors, Renoir applied them in individual touches. It gives the illusion that the composition shimmers with light – Impressionism was particularly concerned with the effect of light.

The financial distress that Renoir found himself in during the mid-1870s had seen his work develop to include depictions of women and children – looking at the painting here, it is obvious that it was a subject in which he excelled. Renoir has adapted the Impressionist principles and applied them to his individual figure works. The colors render the piece fresh and radiant. Many commentators have sought to identify the child, from neighbor's daughters to Mademoiselle Leclere. It is also cited that the painting was created in the backdrop of Monet's garden. None of these claims are substantiated.

Bouquet of Chrysanthemums

(1881)

• Oil on canvas, 25.9 in x 21.9 in (66 cm x 55.6 cm)

Renoir said: "When I paint flowers, I feel free to try out tones and values and worry less about destroying the canvas... I would not do this with a figure painting since there I would care about destroying the work." Still life gave the artist more freedom than he felt he otherwise had and he painted many floral works. They were relatively inexpensive to produce and easier to sell to the public at the time. Apart from the flowers decaying after a period of time there were limited time constraints – as there would have been if painting a figure. This particular work is completely balanced in its color hues.

By the Seashore

(1883)

• Oil on canvas, 36.3 in x 28.5 in (92.1 cm x 72.4 cm)

Renoir, Pierre Auguste (1841-1919): By the Seashore, 1883. New York, Metropolitan Museum of Art. Oil on canvas, 36 1/4 x 28 1/2 in. (92.1 x 72.4 cm).
Inscribed: Signed and dated (lower left): Renoir. 83. H. O. Havemeyer Collection, Bequest of Mrs. H. O. Havemeyer, 1929. Acc.n.: 29.100.125. © 2013.
Image copyright The Metropolitan Museum of Art/Art Resource/Scala, Florence

This exquisite painting was created as Renoir strove from his earlier works of the 1870s to explore something different. He visited Italy between 1881 and 1882 and was exposed to Renaissance art, leading to an emphasizing of contours and modeling. Unlike Monet, who was intent on working en plein air in order to capture the nuances of light and atmosphere, Renoir abandoned the idea that painting outside was necessary. It is thought that *By the Seashore,* painted the year after his return from Italy, was created in the artist's studio with model, Aline Charigot, Renoir's future wife, who had already posed for a number of great artists of the time. In this piece, she is sat in a wicker chair but it is thought the beach in the background is of the Normandy coastline rather than a beach in Guernsey where he spent some time in 1883. He spent about a month in St. Peter Port, admiring the rocks and cliffs, and was taken with the stunning view around Moulin Huet bay. Although he painted the beginnings of 15 works during his stay – which were later finished in his Paris studio – the coasts of Guernsey and Normandy are strikingly similar in parts.

At the time of his travels, to the Normandy coastline (and Guernsey), it is likely that Aline accompanied Renoir. He was struggling with his artistic talents at this time, trying to reconcile the light and color he'd been exposed to through Impressionism and what he believed as its "undisciplined execution." In this piece, the figure and the chair are fetchingly realistic but the background is pure Impressionism. The figure's tilted nose and dark eyebrows were characteristic of Renoir.

Claude Monet
(1875)

• Oil on canvas, 33.5 in x 23.8 in (85 cm x 60.5 cm)

Renoir, Pierre Auguste (1841-1919): Portrait of Claude Monet, 1875. Paris, Musee d'Orsay. © 2013. Photo Scala, Florence

This is a personal portrayal of a fellow painter and close friend, Claude Monet. The figure of the founder of Impressionism is standing in a relaxed pose where the light illuminates the empty room around him. The light penetrates the artist's face and contrasts brilliantly with the dark hues of the figure's clothes. Commentators suggest that the small round hat on Monet's head is as much a halo as it is a piece of clothing and that the long thin leaves which "intrude" all around his head, perhaps, affectionately, "crowning him with laurel."

The work was shown at the second Impressionist exhibition in 1876 and was highly revered by critics and the writer Emile Zola, who said: "His work is worthy of Rembrandt, illuminated by the brilliant light of Velasquez."

Dance at Le Moulin de la Galette

(1876)

• Oil on canvas, 51.6 in x 68.9 in (131 cm x 175 cm)

Renoir, Pierre Auguste (1841-1919): Dance at the Moulin de la Galette, Montmartre, 1876. Paris, Musee d'Orsay. Oil on canvas, 131 x 175 cm. © 2013. Photo Scala, Florence

This extremely important work from the mid-1870s was shown at the Impressionist exhibition of 1877 where Renoir successfully displayed the joyful atmosphere of the popular dance garden on the Butt Montmartre in a study of a moving crowd bathed in natural sunlight. However, he also includes an element of artificial light through the use of lamps, which adorn the garden. Renoir incorporates vibrant, colored brushstrokes but this bustling masterpiece attracted negative comments from critics of the day who just did not understand Impressionism. The piece is rather imposing, but shows a portrayal of popular Parisian life of the time. Moulin de la Galette, near the top of Montmartre, was a characteristic place. This Sunday afternoon dance is one of Renoir's "happier" works. The garden encouraged a local clientele including working girls. Renoir was a frequent visitor as were many of his contemporaries – and some of his friends are seen clearly in the work. Like other artists, both before him and at the time, he combined a number of portraitures within one large work. It is cited that the figure in the striped dress is Estelle, the sister of Renoir's model, Jeanne. Another model, Margot, is seen to the left of the work dancing with Cardenas, the Cuban painter. To the front of the work are Renoir's friends including Georges Rivière, Frank Lamy, and Norbert Goeneutte.

The artist painted a smaller version of the subject – now housed in the Ordrupgard Museum, Copenhagen – as well as another version. Renoir reportedly took an enormous canvas to the garden in order to begin the work, but it is highly likely that it was finished in the studio.

Dance in the City

(1883)

• Oil on canvas, 70.9 in x 35.4 in (180 cm x 90 cm)

Renoir, Pierre Auguste (1841-1919): Dance in the City, 1883. Paris, Musee d'Orsay. Oil on canvas, 180 x 90 cm. © 2013. Photo Scala, Florence

As can be seen from the previous painting, Renoir liked dance scenes and having figures within his works. These two particular works were designed as a pair – poles apart, one based in the city, the other in the rural countryside – one formal, the other casual and relaxed – however, they share the same format. There is elegance in the city dancers, surrounded by a sublime ballroom, while the country dancers look to be having more freedom and fun in the open air, swept away by music that implies an almost disorderly approach, compared to the stiff scene of the first painting.

There are a number of contrasts between the two, from the colors to the coolness of the features of the city dancers and the laughing ones of the country, woman dancer (based on Aline). But, the dance seems incredibly similar. Paul Durand-Ruel owned the two paintings for a number of years, having commissioned three in 1883. The paintings show a marked change in Renoir's technique. There is more simplification here, compared to the vibrant brushstrokes of his earlier works. There is more attention to the actual drawing – said to have been inspired by Renoir's exposure to the works of Raphael in Italy.

The third dance piece was entitled *The Country Dance (La danse à la champagne)*, and shows a young, attractive woman wearing a similar hat (in form and color) and dress to that of the country woman in *Dance in the Country*. However, in the third work, the male dancer has retrieved his hat, casually left on the floor in the second work (although his shoes are different and he has a fairer complexion and hair).

At the time of creating these joyful works, Renoir was content in his domestic life and enjoyed the typical pursuits of the time – including dancing. These pieces tell us that he was enjoying his existence and family life. He chose to

Dance in the Country

(1883)

• Oil on canvas, 70.9 in x 35.4 in (180 cm x 90 cm)

Renoir, Pierre Auguste (1841-1919): Dance in the Country. Paris, Musee d'Orsay. © 2013. Photo Scala, Florence

honor this through dance paintings – indeed, he was becoming more bourgeois. Renoir was known to have a mistrust of knowledgeable women, and while he revered their sensuality and form, he rarely painted them openly enjoying themselves or with a smile. (It is also cited that artists at this time were worried they wouldn't be taken seriously if their figures were smiling.) In *Dance in the Country*, he shows Aline happily smiling as she dances. It is suggested that this is because he did not feel threatened by the working-class seamstress. However, in later works, Renoir put huge emphasis on paintings containing female figures and it was claimed he worked best when surrounded by women.

The Dance series is generally considered one of the most experimental of the artist's career. Like all founding Impressionists, he was greatly influenced by nature and his surroundings. He enjoyed using bright colors and spontaneity – as suggested by the couple in *Dance in the Country* who seem to have spontaneously left their meal to dance to a favorite melody – hence the fallen hat. However, Renoir was said to be increasingly frustrated with the direction the Impressionist movement was taking. His trip to Italy is said to have inspired him to take another look at the past. He wrote: "I will… attain the grandeur and simplicity of the ancient painters," and during the next six years from 1882 onward, experimented with his art. His art began to demonstrate a tighter style and he strove for classicism. This was often referred to as his Ingres Period, due to his focus on his drawing technique and the accentuated outlines of his figures. Renoir had a dedication to joyful pieces, making him less fashionable than his contemporaries – particularly with critics. This was further hampered by his move away from Impressionism, which left him without a movement to fully belong to.

Diana

(1867)

• Oil on canvas, 78.5 in x 50.9 in (199.5 cm x 129.5 cm)

Diane. Deesse de la chasse dans la mythologie Digitale representee sous les traits d'une femme nue avec fourrure, arc et fleche pres d'un chevreuil mort. Peinture de Pierre Auguste RENOIR (1841-1919), 1867. Impressionnisme. Huile sur toile Washington.National Gallery of Art. © 2013. White Images/Scala, Florence

Lise Tréhot, Renoir's mistress, posed for this piece created in 1867. It was Renoir's way of painting a study of a nude – a traditional mainstay of the academic art world. He later admitted that the bow, dead animal, and deerskin were added to transform Lise into Diana, goddess of hunting, as he considered the painting fairly "improper." He felt that the woman's voluptuous nudity would be more acceptable to the Salon. They rejected it, however, perhaps because despite Renoir's intention to do otherwise, it still closely resembled a real woman rather than a mystical, ancient heroine. The creation of the work was one of the few times that Renoir used a palette knife to apply pigments – a favorite technique of Gustave Courbet, the realist painter, who seems to have influenced the French artist in this work at least. Some commentators believe that this is one of the most important works ever painted by Renoir.

Fernand Halphen as a Boy

(1880)

• Oil on canvas, 18.1 in x 14.9 in (46 cm x 38 cm)

Renoir, Pierre Auguste (1841-1919): Fernand Halphen enfant. 1880. Paris, Musee d'Orsay. © 2013. Gaspart/Scala, Florence

This beautiful painting shows exactly why Renoir was such an expert figure and portraiture painter. His first public success in this area came with a family portrait of *Madame Charpentier and her Children*, which was accepted for the Salon exhibition in 1869. The lady herself, whose husband was an eminent publisher, was instrumental in many of Renoir's early portrait commissions. Mr. and Mrs. Halphen were influential, wealthy Parisians who commissioned him to paint this exquisite portrait of their son, Fernand (1872-1917). He was the youngest of five children. He was a talented child who won the second Grand Prix de Rome for composition in 1896. He dedicated his life to music before dying during the First World War (1914-1918) on the battlefield in his mid-forties. The Halphens obviously didn't think much of the portrait because they gave it to Fernand's former governess. Art dealer Jos Kessel bought the painting and sold it to collector, Charles Pacquement. He in turn, suffering from trauma after his own time on the battlefield during the Great War, kindly gave the painting to Fernand's widow. His son, Georges Halphen, offered the portrait to the Musée d'Orsay in 1995.

Field of Banana Trees

(1881)

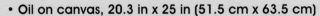

• Oil on canvas, 20.3 in x 25 in (51.5 cm x 63.5 cm)

Renoir, Pierre Auguste (1841-1919): Un champ de bananiers. 1881. Paris, Musee d'Orsay. Peinture. Dim. 0.51 x 0.63 m. © 2013. White Images/Scala, Florence

Paul Durand-Ruel was Renoir's greatest supporter. He regularly bought paintings from him, enabling Renoir to travel more extensively than he ever had before. It would also help him to finalize his artistic training. He first visited Algeria – following in the footsteps of Delacroix whom he greatly admired – and he found it an intense experience where he was overwhelmed by the vibrant colors and extraordinary nature. It even prompted him to create a number of landscapes, which are rare among his works.

This piece is the Essai Garden in Hamma, showing a field of banana trees – luxurious vegetation in a truly tropical theme. He has used an incredibly subtle brushwork to achieve this magnificent work, which was presented many years later, in 1895, at the Salon for the Society of Orientalist Painters. It achieved a fair amount of critical acclaim.

Frédéric Bazille

(1867)

- **Oil on canvas, 41.3 in x 28.9 in (105 cm x 73.5 cm)**

Renoir, Pierre Auguste (1841-1919): Portrait of Bazille, 1867. Paris, Musee d'Orsay. © 2013. Photo Scala, Florence

Bazille had a studio in rue Visconti, Paris, which he willingly shared with Renoir, Monet, Sisley, and Manet. In 1867, Renoir created this portrait of Bazille at work painting *The Heron with Wings Unfurled*. He includes a snowscape in the background in tribute to Monet – who in turn painted Renoir's portrait – and Manet would eventually own the piece.

The painting of Bazille shows the artist hard at work, slouched forward in the chair while his feet are propped, slightly to the side and crossed. He is wearing a grey suit and espadrilles with red laces, and Renoir chooses for the gray, beige, and brown to dominate the piece – in the style of Manet. Surrounding Bazille is a plethora of paintings covering the studio wall. Some face inward, some outward. The artist had enrolled at the studio of Charles Gleyre in 1862, but by the time of this painting, he, Renoir, Sisley, and Monet had all begun to take a new direction within their works. Working together in Bazille's studio in 1867 was the start of sharing space and direction while supporting and encouraging each other.

Gabrielle and Jean

(c. 1895)

• Oil on canvas, 25.6 in x 21.3 in (65 cm x 54 cm)

Renoir, Pierre Auguste (1841-1919): Gabrielle and Jean. Paris, Orangerie. © 2013. Photo Scala, Florence

Renoir was 53 years old when Jean, his second son, was born in 1894. By this time, he was a reasonably successful artist but he was still plagued by doubts about his ability. He had also been suffering from arthritis for about two years when he painted this beautiful work of his child and 16-year-old Fernande-Gabrielle Renard, who had been hired to help with Renoir's growing family. It shows a joyful scene. Family provided Renoir with a great deal of joy and happiness, which began to take shape in his art around the time of Jean's birth.

The figures here appear to be unaware that they are being observed – they are totally immersed in the activity they share. However, it would have been difficult to keep a baby's attention for long and it is likely that rather than being quite the spontaneous pose that is suggested, it is likely that initial sketches would have had to have been quickly drawn. It is a gentle and engaging portrait of love and happiness. Renoir used Gabrielle and Jean for his models on many occasions. Gabrielle remained with the Renoir family for 18 years. She was nursemaid, housekeeper, model, and studio assistant. She was undoubtedly Renoir's most important model and he painted her in around 200 paintings. In many, she is posed nude and eventually this brought things to a head with Aline who dismissed the woman in 1912. However, Gabrielle returned to the household following Aline's death in 1915.

In this particular painting of Gabrielle and Jean, Renoir carefully paints an unruly lock of hair falling over the young girl's face. It shows the intimacy and love that surrounded the work. This was to last a lifetime – Gabrielle and her eventual husband, the American artist Conrad Slade, moved to Beverly Hills in 1921 at the invitation of Jean Renoir, by then a successful moviemaker and director. Gabrielle remained in the United States until her death at the age of 81 in 1959.

Gabrielle with a Rose

(1911)

• Oil on canvas, 18.5 in x 21.9 in (47 cm x 55.5 cm)

Renoir, Pierre Auguste (1841-1919): Gabrielle with a Rose. Paris, Musee d'Orsay. © 2013. Photo Scala, Florence

Renoir painted this beautiful portrayal of Gabrielle in 1911, just eight years before he died. Some commentators have observed that while Renoir returned to the Impressionism he had favored earlier in his career, he also returned to the basics of the great masters of Rubens and Titian. His mastery of color in this portrait is simply breathtaking.

By this time, his arthritis was particularly crippling. However, he continued to work despite the huge pain he suffered and was particularly keen on models – especially Gabrielle – whose skin "took the light." According to experts, Renoir was as interested in the beauty of the skin and the flesh itself as he was the woman's body. Here, Gabrielle holds a pink rose to her ear; old photographs show the rose was made from paper.

Jeanne Samary in Low-Cut Dress

(1877)

• Oil on canvas, 22 in x 18.5 in (56 cm x 47 cm)

Renoir, Pierre Auguste (1841-1919): Jeanne Samary in Low-Cut Dress. Moscow, Pushkin Museum. © 2013. Photo Scala, Florence

This beautifully exquisite portrait of Jeanne Samary is one of three for which she posed for Renoir. The famous actress who worked in the Comédie Française was greatly admired for her beauty. Renoir exclaimed that her skin "illuminated everything around it."

Painted while Jeanne Samary was in her 20s, this piece has strong links to Impressionism and the color within it has great importance. The brushstrokes are swift and undefined. *Jeanne Samary in Low-Cut Dress* is considered a Renoir masterpiece of Impressionism. Renoir met the actress in 1877. Of his three portraits of the actress, this is possibly the most engaging. Each of the works is different in their composition, color, and size.

Julie Manet (also known as Child with Cat)
(1887)

• Oil on canvas, 25.6 in x 21.3 in (65 cm x 54 cm)

Renoir, Pierre Auguste (1841-1919): Portrait of Julie Manet or little girl with cat. Paris, Musee d'Orsay. © 2013. Photo Scala, Florence

Julie Manet, niece of Manet, was the daughter of Eugène Manet and his wife, Berthe Morisot. The couple was devoted to Renoir and loved his works. They became close to him in the late 1880s and commissioned this portrait in 1887.

There were a number of preparatory drawings made for the painting, which Renoir painted in small sections – not his usual preferred way of working. His Ingres Period was little understood by some of his friends and close acquaintances, but Berthe Morisot particularly liked his works during this time. The portrait – described by the sitter herself in later years as a good likeness – is a gentle and serene work that captures the sensitivity and affection of the artist in the young girl.

La Grenouillère

(1869)

• Oil on canvas, 26.2 in x 31.9 in (66.5 cm x 81 cm)

Renoir's *La Grenouillère* has all the ingredients of Impressionism. The individual details are waived in favor of the overall piece while the glitter of the sun reflects the movement of the water. This is helped by the fragmented brushstrokes on the pond, which are captivating, all held together by the exquisite light illuminating the water bringing it to life. It was at this time – during the summer of 1869 – that Renoir and Monet chose to work side-by-side en plein air. They were drawn to the area by its reputation for beauty and tranquility.

La Loge
(1874)

• Oil on canvas, 31.5 in x 25 in (80 cm x 63.5 cm)

La Loge. Couple de spectateurs a l'opera avec des jumelles. Peinture de Pierre Auguste Renoir (1841-1919), 1874. Art impressioniste. Huile sur toile. Dim: 80 x 63.5 cm. Londres, Courtauld Institute Galleries. © 2013. White Images/Scala, Florence

La Loge, 1874, is a celebrated work from the Courtauld Collection and one of the most important Impressionist works. The theater in Paris was becoming increasingly popular in the 19th century and began to dominate cultural society. Everybody who was anybody had to be seen at the theater and Renoir was no exception. It was a place to show wealth and to wear the latest expensive fashions. Business was carried out, deals made, and hands shaken. Family announcements were made. It was a place where status and relationships went on public display and Renoir captured this perfectly in this piece, shown at the first Impressionist exhibition in 1874. He shows the audience a moment of contemporary life in Paris. The figures were posed by Renoir's brother Edmond and the well-known Montmartre model, Nini gueule en raie. While it is a creative work of Impressionism, Renoir flouts the rules by using black and giving less importance to the light and illumination. He eventually sold the work to art dealer, Le père Martin, for 425 francs when no other buyer was interested. The reason for this exacting sum was that the 33-year-old artist needed the money for his rent.

Works like this became important commentaries on contemporary life. The fact that the male figure is using his opera glasses to look at a member of the audience in the balcony above, combined with the flowers and fan, suggest Renoir's eye for contemporary detail.

Lise with a Parasol

(1867)

- Oil on canvas, 72.4 in x 45.3 in (184 cm x 115 cm)

Here, Lise Tréhot is portrayed in the natural setting of a park. Completed in 1867, the figure appears to be taking a summer stroll under the shade of her parasol. It was widely praised by Zola at the Paris Salon in 1868 for its modern approach. As already stated in an earlier work, *Diana*, 1867, Lise was Renoir's mistress at this time. They lived together until around 1872. She was a model for a number of his early paintings.

Luncheon of the Boating Party
(1881)

• Oil on canvas, 51.3 in x 69.1 in (130.20 cm x 175.60 cm)

Luncheon of the Boating Party, 1881, by Pierre-Auguste Renoir (1841-1919), oil on canvas, 130.30 x 175.60 cm. Washington DC, Phillips Collection.
© 2013. DeAgostini Picture Library/Scala, Florence

Also known as *Le déjeuner des canotiers, Luncheon of the Boating Party*, 1881, was created at the height of Renoir's Impressionist career and considered one of the most important canvases of the time. It shows a group of the artist's friends relaxing over a meal and drinks on the Maison Fournaise in Chatou, France. Aline can be seen in the foreground on the left, playing with a small dog. She appears to be the only protagonist who is not joining in the general conversation. It is almost as if the artist is expressing his feelings for her by setting her apart from the other figures. It is suggested that her status is also elevated from the others by the vibrant colors of her hat. One of Renoir's wealthy patrons, Gustave Caillebotte, is seen in the foreground wearing a straw hat, while artist Paul Lhote, Charles Ephrussi (editor of the *Gazette des Beaux-Arts*), and poet Jules Laforgue are also included. Ellen Andree, Jeanne Samary, and Angele Legault (all actresses) also figure as do Baron Raoul Barbier, former mayor of colonial Saigon, and the children of the owner, Louise-Alphonsine Fournaise as well as her brother Alphonse Fournaise Jr.

Renoir fell in love with Chatou in 1868 where he discovered the Restaurant Fournaise. He frequented the eatery regularly and produced around 30 canvases of Chatou, both within the restaurant and the surrounding areas. This particular piece is a snapshot of everyday life. Renoir had intended to show the work at the Paris Salon, but Paul Durand-Ruel purchased it for the seventh Impressionist exhibition. Zola had long criticized the Impressionists and challenged them to produce works that were more completed modern-day paintings. Many believe that this painting was executed in response to this challenge, while others cite that Renoir painted it to highlight Degas's comment that Impressionists could not expect to be a part of the official Salon and show their works at the Impressionist exhibitions. Around this time, Renoir, Monet, and others were excluded from the Impressionist movement, while Degas introduced younger artists to take their places. In his attempt to reinforce his position, Renoir blended various traditional categories of painting – still life, landscape, portraiture, and genre. It is truly a timeless masterpiece, engaging and full of enchantment. The work took Renoir six months, with a number of compositional changes, including the addition of the striped awning.

Madame Georges Charpentier
(née Marguérite-Louise Lemonnier, 1848-1904) and Her Children, Georgette-Berthe (1872-1945) and Paul-Émile-Charles (1875-1895)

(1878)

• Oil on canvas, 60.5 in x 74.9 in (153.7 cm x 190.2 cm)

Renoir, Pierre Auguste (1841-1919): Madame Georges Charpentier (Marguérite-Louise Lemonnier, 1848-1904) and Her Children, Georgette-Berthe (1872-1945) and Paul-Émile-Charles (1875-1895), 1878. New York, Metropolitan Museum of Art. Oil on canvas, 60 1/2 x 74 7/8 in. (153.7 x 190.2 cm). Inscribed: Signed and dated (lower right): Renoir. 78. Catharine Lorillard Wolfe Collection, Wolfe Fund, 1907. Acc.n.: 07.122 © 2013. Image copyright The Metropolitan Museum of Art/Art Resource/Scala, Florence

By the time Renoir reached the year 1879 he chose to decline participating in the fourth Impressionist exhibition and opted instead to return to the more traditional annual Paris Salon. His portraiture of *Madame Charpentier and Her Children,* which would result in further commissions, was exhibited at the Salon that year to great acclaim. Publisher Georges Charpentier had commissioned Renoir to paint his family. Marguérite Charpentier, seated by her three-year-old son Paul, wears a Worth gown. The child, in keeping with the fashion of the day, had not yet had his hair cut. He was also dressed in clothes that matched those of his sister Georgette, who sits with the family dog. Madame Charpentier was pleased with the painting and used her considerable influence to ensure that it was given pride of place in a prominent spot at the exhibition. She then introduced the painter to many of her friends, leading to further commissions. It was one of five works exhibited that year by Renoir for the Salon. This particular piece – painted in payment for the times the family had helped him financially – was one of his most successful works. The family is shown in the small drawing room of their mansion. Incidentally, Paul Charpentier was the godson of the celebrated writer Zola. The painting was eventually acquired by the state and Renoir was wheeled into the Louvre several months before his death in 1919 to see the work, alongside his other celebrated masterpieces, for the last time.

Maternity (also called Child at the breast)
(1885)

• Oil on canvas, 36 in x 28.3 in (91.5 cm x 72 cm)

Renoir, Pierre Auguste (1841-1919): Madame Renoir with her son, Pierre. Paris, Musee d'Orsay. © 2013. Photo Scala, Florence

This magnificent painting is of Aline feeding the couple's firstborn son, Pierre. Following Pierre's birth, Renoir created a number of oil paintings and a series of drawings of Aline feeding the baby. Pierre is shown clutching his foot in all the poses. Commentators – looking at the age of the child – believe the composition was produced in September or October 1885.

While the figures are perfectly created, the background is merely suggested. Under the glaze, the pencil lines can still be clearly seen. This piece is typical of the Ingres Period when Renoir became intensely interested in drawing. It shows a clear line and relates closely to traditional classical Italian painting. It could be seen as a modern-day Madonna and child.

Fatherhood greatly interested Renoir in painting children – up to this point he had only been commissioned to paint them by wealthy patrons. The introduction of his own children in his compositions suggests that he finally came to terms with his own background and class and, if analyzed carefully, shows the artist's ideas on raising his own sons. The birth of Pierre prompted Renoir to settle down in a way he had managed to avoid up to 1885. The fascination he had for his sons' skin continued when Jean and Claude were born in 1894 and 1901 respectively.

Moulin Huet Bay, Guernsey

(1883)

- **Oil on canvas, 11.5 in x 21.3 in (29.2 cm x 54 cm)**

This beautiful depiction of the stunning Moulin Huet Bay on the Channel Island of Guernsey shows three figures in the foreground and the rocks of Les Tas de Pois d'Amont to the left. The rocks on the right are said to be Cradle Rock, "La Surtaut." The work was produced during Renoir's visit to idyllic Guernsey in September 1883. He created around 15 paintings during his time on the historic island, all showing views of the bay and beach at the east end of the rocky south coast. Paul Durand-Ruel is believed to have bought the painting, which was acquired by the National Gallery in London in 1954. Guernsey celebrated Renoir's visit and landscapes on commemorative stamps in 1983.

Oarsmen at Chatou

(1879)

- Oil on canvas, 31.9 in x 39.4 in (81.2 cm x 100.2 cm)

Renoir, Pierre Auguste (1841-1919): Les canotiers a Chatou en 1879. 1879. Washington DC, National Gallery of Art. Peinture. Dim: 0.81 x 1.00 m.© 2013. White Images/Scala, Florence

Renoir loved Chatou, just a few miles upstream from Argenteuil (where Monet spent a great deal of time painting from his boat studio). While Argenteuil was renowned for its Parisian visitors, who enjoyed watching the sailing boats and the races that ensued, Chatou was better known for its rowing. The two-person boats were designed for relaxation. The rower sat facing the passenger, who controlled the rudder with ropes. The rower in the boat here is possibly Renoir's brother, Edmond. It is thought that the man standing on the bank is Gustave Caillebotte who was a rowing enthusiast. Aline is suggested by many as the woman in the painting, while the man facing the audience is not known.

This painting is stunning for the sheer brilliance of the shimmering water, the orange hues used for the boat and its reflection, and its overall use of color. The sunlight that hits the water in the left-hand section of the piece is genius.

Pink and Blue (also known as *Alice and Elisabeth Cahen d'Anvers*)

(1881)

- Oil on canvas, 46.9 in x 29.1 in (119 cm x 74 cm)

Pink and blue, 1881, by Pierre-Auguste Renoir (1841-1919), oil on canvas, 119 x 74 cm. Sao Paulo, Museu de Arte de Sao Paulo. © 2013. DeAgostini Picture Library/Scala, Florence

These beautiful little girls, with their pink and blue sashes that match their socks, were created in this portraiture by Renoir when they were six and five. Alice Cahen d'Anvers (born 1876) and her sister, Elisabeth (born 1874), were the daughters of Louis Raphael Cahen d'Anvers, a prominent French banker. The family was among one of the wealthiest in Paris at the time.

Renoir was commissioned to paint a number of portraits for the family, whom he met through the proprietor of the *Gazette des Beaux-Arts,* Charles Ephrussi. He had already painted the older sister, Irene, in an earlier portrait so, originally, Renoir was to paint the two younger girls separately, but it was decided to paint them together. The portrait took a number of sittings, which caused the small children much boredom. Alice died at the age of 89 in Nice in 1965. Her sister Elisabeth, twice divorced, was sent to Auschwitz in March 1944 due to her Jewish descent. She died on the journey aged 69.

Pont Neuf, Paris

(1872)

• Oil on canvas, 29.6 in x 36.9 in (75.3 cm x 93.7 cm)

Renoir, Pierre Auguste (1841-1919): Le Pont Neuf a Paris en 1872. 1872. Washington DC, National Gallery of Art. Peinture. Dim. 0.75 x 0.93 m. © 2013. White Images/Scala, Florence

This exquisite work was created at a time when Impressionism was taking shape. While Renoir was particularly renowned for his figures – and especially nudes – his landscapes are no less stunning. The figures here are created with quick brushstrokes and the finer detail is lost under the illuminating sun. The effect of light on the senses does exactly what Renoir – and other Impressionist painters – aimed for it to do. The blue hues for the shadows are a clever touch of a "busy" crowd crossing the Pont Neuf in Paris. It is the oldest bridge in the city. Notice the man in the straw boater carrying the cane – he appears twice. He is Edmond Renoir, who under the watchful eye of his brother was stopping people to chat. While they paused to have a brief conversation, Renoir was able to sketch them from a nearby café.

Cityscapes were long considered to be a staple of landscapes in general and, in cities such as Paris, they were particularly popular. Renoir had a passion for urban life and the changes that took place in Paris throughout the architectural developments, as well as the people that bustled along the widened streets. Baron Haussmann was modernizing Paris at a time when Impressionists were keen to paint the changing landscape. Under Napoleon, the small, winding streets and alleyways were opened out into wide boulevards and sweeping vistas so favorable in Paris today. In this piece, Renoir concentrates on the frenetic pace of the vibrant city with rapid brushwork.

Richard Wagner

(1882)

• Oil on canvas, 20.9 in x 18.1 in (53 cm x 46 cm)

Renoir, Pierre Auguste (1841-1919): Portrait de Richard Wagner (1813-1883). 19 eme siecle. Paris, Musee d'Orsay. Peinture. Dim: 0.53 x 0.46m. © 2013. White Images/Scala, Florence

Wagner and Renoir met in Palermo, Italy, in 1882. Renoir was passionate about music and particularly loved the works of the German composer who had just finished composing *Parsifal*.

Writing to a friend on January 15, 1882, Renoir states that Wagner was a friendly man who shared a few drinks with him. They met the following day for a short sitting and Renoir writes: "He was very happy, but very nervous." The sitting took about 35 minutes and Wagner apparently became "stiff," which led Renoir to create a "Protestant Minister," as Wagner described himself on seeing the portrait. Renoir had been in Italy at the time of the meeting to study the works of Titian in Florence. Some commentators suggest that having been an avid follower of Wagner, Renoir was less enchanted with the composer after their meeting.

The Bathers

(c. 1918-1919)

• Oil on canvas, 43.3 in x 62.9 in (110 cm x 160 cm)

Renoir, Pierre Auguste (1841-1919): Bathers. Paris, Musee d'Orsay. © 2013. Photo Scala, Florence

This magnificent work was created after Renoir returned to one of his favorite subjects – nudes en plein air – in 1910, although this came later, just prior to his death. The nudes negate the need for commentary on modern life. They are timeless in their appeal and represent nature at its most vibrant. It was a time, toward the end of his life, when the artist returned to a period of experimentation. The models posed in the garden at Les Collettes, Renoir's property in Cagnes-sur-Mer in the South of France. Against a backdrop of olive trees, he depicts five nudes relaxing. Two are shown in the foreground, while the other three are seen in the stream. One of the models is Andrée Hessling, who became the first wife of Jean Renoir. This work has a classical feel of the Italians and Greeks. The models are sensual and the colors are carefully crafted. The painting shows no sign of the pain and suffering of the artist who was greatly afflicted at this time. Renoir's three sons presented the painting to the state in 1923. It is now housed in the Musée d'Orsay in Paris.

The Boy with the Cat

(1868)

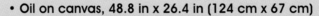

• Oil on canvas, 48.8 in x 26.4 in (124 cm x 67 cm)

Renoir, Pierre-Auguste (1841-1919). Young Boy and Cat; Le Jeune Garcon au Chat. London, Private Coll. Oil on canvas. 124 x 67 cm.
© 2013. Christies' Images, London/Scala, Florence

The young nude boy's identity in this painting is unknown. He is seen here cuddling a cat. It was composed at the beginning of Renoir's career and marked a turning point in his work, with its cold color harmonies probably attributable to the influence of Manet and Courbet. A public auction in 1992 saw the painting go to the Musée d'Orsay. Renoir was keen to include cats in his works as a way of introducing a relaxed informality.

The Garden in the rue Cortot, Montmartre
(1876)

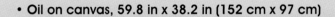

• Oil on canvas, 59.8 in x 38.2 in (152 cm x 97 cm)

Renoir, Pierre Auguste (1841-1919): Le jardin rue Cortot a Montmartre. 1876. Pittsburgh, Institute Museum of Art. Peinture. © 2013. White Images/Scala, Florence

The captured light effects in this work give it the classic Impressionist immediacy and spontaneity. Private gardens offered Impressionists a wealth of subject material from which to draw inspiration, and this garden in the rue Cortot, once part of the grounds of an 18th-century chateau, was no exception. Renoir discovered the garden between 1875 and 1876 and soon after rented a cottage on the street. The garden became not just his subject, but also his outdoor studio. Commentators cite that the dahlias in the foreground, shown in all their blazing glory, are the main subject of the painting with their brilliant colors and growth. The long-neglected garden was perfect for the varied brushwork of the Impressionist's style and allowed a freedom and expressiveness not always found in idyllic landscapes, cityscapes, and seascapes.

It is thought that the two men in the background are Monet and Sisley, shrouded in light in contrast to the shade that seems to overwhelm the rest of the garden.

The Mosque

(1881)

The Mosque, or Arab Festival, 1881. Artist: Pierre-Auguste Renoir. From the collection of the Musee d'Orsay, Paris, France. © 2013. Photo Art Media/Heritage Images/Scala, Florence

Set in Algiers in the ancient Turkish ramparts, this masterful portrayal of the local mosque shows a joyful crowd of people swarming around a group of musicians. The cupolas and minarets of the Kasbah are overlooking the Mediterranean Sea. For European painters, images of ceremonies or festivals far from home were popular subject matter. Renoir uses a rapid brushwork and uses a great deal of freedom to compose this piece – even on the simple dashes of color for some of the faces in the crowd. It is a bold composition, which presents a scene of happiness from the French-African colony of Algeria (where he stayed between 1881 and 1882). While here, Renoir created more than 24 stunning pieces incorporating the exotic.

The Skiff (La Yole)

(1875)

• Oil on canvas, 27.9 in x 36.2 in (71 cm x 92 cm)

Renoir, Pierre Auguste (1841-1919): The Skiff (La Yole), 1875. London, National Gallery. Oil on canvas, 71 x 92 cm. Bought, 1982. Acc.n.: 1567.
© 2013. Copyright The National Gallery, London/Scala, Florence

It is believed that this work is of Chatou, one of Renoir's favorite places, to the west of Paris on the Seine. The orange hue of the skiff against the blues and greens balances perfectly within the painting; he applied the oils with small brushstrokes, revealing emotion and Impressionism rather than a realistic picturesque scene. Renoir typically used fragmented or broken brushstrokes – known as "taches" ("spots") in French.

The Swing

(1876)

- **Oil on canvas, 36.2 in x 28.7 in (92 cm x 73 cm)**

Renoir, Pierre Auguste (1841-1919): La balancoire. Jeanne est la modele sur la balancoire du Jardin Corot a Montmartre. A gauche pres de l'arbre, Norbert Goeneutte, peintre francais (1854-1894). 1876. Paris, Musee d'Orsay. Peinture. Dim. 0.92 x 0.73 m. © 2013. White Images/Scala, Florence

This beautiful depiction encapsulates calmness and serenity in an everyday activity. A young woman stands by a swing, watched by a man and a little girl as she chats to the man facing her. It is a snapshot of life. It is suggested that the young woman looks away from the men as if embarrassed. The four figures in the foreground are balanced by a larger group toward the background of the work. This painting was worked on in parallel with *The Ball at the Moulin de la Galette,* in the summer of 1876. The models for the piece are Edmond Renoir, the artist Robert Goeneutte, and Jeanne, a young woman from Montmartre. All the models also appear in the sister painting which has the same carefree atmosphere as this work. Renoir expertly captures the light effects through the sunlight, dappled by the foliage. The effects are highlighted by pale colors: notice the clothing and the ground. The painting was shown at the third Impressionist exhibition in 1877 and, despite annoying the critics, was bought by Gustave Caillebotte, who also bought *The Ball at the Moulin de la Galette.*

The work was painted in the garden of Renoir's patron, the publisher, Charpentier.

The Two Sisters (On the Terrace)

(1881)

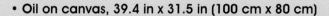

• Oil on canvas, 39.4 in x 31.5 in (100 cm x 80 cm)

Renoir, Pierre Auguste (1841-1919): On the Terrace, 1881. Chicago (IL), Art Institute of Chicago. © 2013. Photo Scala, Florence

This exquisite work came at the peak of Renoir's career in 1881 and has proved to be one of his most popular paintings. It gained its second title – *On the Terrace* – from Paul Durand-Ruel, who remained the work's only owner for many years. It was painted in Chatou in Restaurant Fournaise, on the same terrace as *Luncheon of the Boating Party*, 1881. It was also the same spot that he had chosen a year earlier for his *Girl on a Balcony*. This work, however, is more complicated than the earlier work and Renoir chose to sit the two figures close to the railings next to a tub of flowers. Both works are achingly delicate. Here, the light glistens on the water. The painting was included in the seventh Impressionist exhibition in the spring of 1882, alongside *Luncheon of the Boating Party* and three other pieces. The older girl has been established as Jeanne Darlot (1863-1914) who was 18 years old at the time. It is not known who the younger child was.

The Umbrellas

(c. 1881-1886)

• Oil on canvas, 70.9 in x 45.2 in (180.3 cm x 114.9 cm)

Renoir, Pierre Auguste (1841-1919): The Umbrellas, about 1881-86. London, National Gallery. Oil on canvas, 180.3 x 114.9 cm. Sir Hugh Lane Bequest, 1917. Acc.n.: 6110.
© 2013. Copyright The National Gallery, London/Scala, Florence

This beautiful painting shows Paris in the rain on a busy street. That some of the figures are "cut off" the canvas makes it more like a photographic record of Parisian life. Even the hands of the protagonists do not immediately capture the audience's attention. It was an unconventional arrangement that Renoir (and Degas) particularly enjoyed experimenting with. When he began painting this piece, Renoir was still using the loose and fragmented brushstrokes that signaled his Impressionist traits. However, he was beginning to feel increasingly disillusioned with the techniques he was employing and made a concerted move toward his Ingres Period, a move that would take him to the past and the more traditional and conventional artist techniques. This piece shows a new attention to design – the umbrellas of the title form a linear pattern unassociated with Impressionism. There is also great care with form taken in the umbrella handles, the girl's hoop, and the basket in the foreground. There is also a Cézanne-like treatment of the tree which, combined with other influences, suggests that the work was painted and reworked a number of times or completed over an extended period. Sir Hugh Lane bought the work from Paul Durand-Ruel in 1892 and left it to the Tate Gallery, London in 1917. It was transferred a short distance to the National Gallery in 1935.

Young Girls at the Piano

(1892)

• **Oil on canvas, 45.7 in x 35.4 in (116 cm x 90 cm)**

Renoir, Pierre Auguste (1841-1919): Jeunes filles au piano. 1892. Paris, Musee d'Orsay. Peinture. Dim. 1.16 x 0.9 m. © 2013. White Images/Scala, Florence

Although ridiculed by Degas, Renoir liked painting young girls and children with particularly round faces. The dark-haired girl in this piece shows a typically round, Renoir, face. Friends of the artist took exception that the state had never bought any paintings from him. Roger Marx, from the Beaux Arts administration, and Stéphane Mallarmé, an admirer of Renoir, began the fight in 1892 to bring the works of the Impressionists to national museums. Following an informal commission *Young Girls at the Piano*, 1892, found its way to the Musée du Luxembourg. There are at least three other compositions using the same subject, two of which remain in private collections while the third is in the Met in New York. There is also a sketch in oils and a pastel version (also contained within a private collection). This is unsurprising. Renoir had great doubts about his artistic abilities and spent a great deal of time reworking his paintings over extended periods. It is also possible that, like Monet, he wished to create a series of works of the same subject. Renoir had a particular interest in middle-class entertainment – the piano remained at the center of these activities as a popular and respectable leisure pursuit for young women. As the painting was commissioned for the new museum in Luxembourg, Renoir was well aware that his work would come under much scrutiny. Here he also creates a comfortable, bourgeois atmosphere in his desire to be respected and admired.

Renoir

In The 21st Century

(PA Photos)

■ **ABOVE:** Paintings by Pierre-Auguste Renoir are seen during a press preview at the Philadelphia Museum of Art.

Places to view the works of Renoir

AUSTRIA
Galerie Belvedere, Vienna

BRAZIL
Museu de Arte, Sao Paulo
Museu de Arte Assis Chateaubriand, Sao Paulo

CANADA
Art Gallery of Ontario, Toronto

CZECH REPUBLIC
Narodni Galerie, Prague

FRANCE
Musée d'Orsay, Paris
Musée de l'Orangerie, Paris
Durand-Ruel Collection, Paris
Musée des Beaux Arts, Lyon
Musée National Picasso, Paris

Galerie Daniel Malingue, Paris
Musée des Beaux Arts, Grenoble
Musée des Beaux-Arts Andre Malraux, Le Havre
Museum of Palace of Versailles, Paris
Musée des Beaux Arts, Bordeaux
Musée des Beaux Arts, Rouen

GERMANY
Hamburger Kunsthalle, Hamburg
Stadel Museum, Frankfurt
Gemaldegalerie, Berlin
Museum Folkwang, Essen

ISRAEL
The Israel Museum, Jerusalem

JAPAN
Museum of Art, Hiroshima
National Museum of Western Art, Tokyo
Bridgestone Museum of Art, Tokyo
Fuji Art Museum, Tokyo

NETHERLANDS
Kroller-Mueller Museum, Otterlo

NORWAY
Nasjonalgalleriet, Oslo

RUSSIA
Pushkin Museum of Fine Arts, Moscow
The State Hermitage Museum, St. Petersburg

SPAIN
Thyssen-Bornemisza Museum, Madrid

SWEDEN
National Museum, Stockholm

SWITZERLAND
Oskar Reinhart Museum, Winterthur
Kunstmuseum, Winterthur
E. G. Buhrie Foundation Collection, Zurich
Kunsthaus, Zurich
Kunstmuseum, Basel

UK
Art Gallery and Museums, Aberdeen
Courtauld Institute of Art, London
Barber Institute of Fine Arts, Birmingham
National Gallery, London
Fitzwilliam Museum, Cambridge
Art Gallery and Museum, Glasgow
National Gallery of Scotland, Edinburgh

USA
Boston Museum of Fine Arts, Massachusetts
Art Institute of Chicago, Illinois
Barnes Foundation, Merion
Metropolitan Museum of Art, New York
Cleveland Museum of Art, Ohio
National Gallery of Art, Washington, DC
Fine Arts Museums of San Francisco, California
J. Paul Getty Museum, Los Angeles
Museum of Fine Arts, Houston
Philadelphia Museum of Art, Pennsylvania
Wadsworth Atheneum, Hartford
Sterling and Francine Clark Art Museum, Massachusetts
Portland Art Museum, Oregon
Carnegie Museum of Art, Pittsburgh
Fogg Art Museum at Harvard University, Massachusetts
Phillips Collection, Washington, DC
Minneapolis Institute of Arts, Minnesota

Kreeger Museum, Washington, DC
Solomon R. Guggenheim Museum, New York
Columbus Museum of Art, Ohio
Frick Collection, New York
Detroit Institute of Arts, Michigan
Albright-Knox Art Gallery, Buffalo
Dallas Museum of Art, Texas
Saint Louis Art Museum, Missouri
Yale University Art Gallery, Connecticut
Indianapolis Museum of Art, Indiana
Fred Jones Jr. Museum of Art at University of Oklahoma, Oklahoma
Worcester Art Museum, Massachusetts
Rhode Island Museum of Art, Providence
Cincinnati Art Museum, Ohio

Renoir at home in the 21st century

Although closed for refurbishment for a time, the Musée Renoir, located at Cagnes-sur-Mer, reopened to the public in 2013. It was the last home of the artist and is preserved with its original furniture and decoration. Featured are two artist's studios, 11 paintings, and virtually all Renoir's sculptures, preparatory sketches, old photographs, lithographs, and personal possessions. The permanent collection was transferred to Château-Musée, also found in Cagnes-sur-Mer.

Renoir's legacy

Renoir created several thousands of paintings, and his output – like his contemporaries – was prolific. His figures are easier to relate to and his works have an engaging quality that has rendered the French artist one of the most well known in art history. This has added to the appeal of Renoir, who leaves a legacy that endures well into the 21st century.

Great-grandson of Renoir, Alexandre Renoir, himself a great artist, said in 2012: "He believed there were enough dark things in the world and he did not want to add to them. He wanted his paintings to inspire peace and enliven someone's life." Renoir's most innovative and fertile decades of his career came toward the end of his life. His art was timeless, enticing, and his artistic talents are worthy of comparison with the old masters such as Titian, Rubens, and Raphael – the artists he revered – and his fluid brushstrokes and use of color surely make his works a remarkable legacy for admirers of the 21st century. He won

■ **ABOVE:** Visitors look at the work *Allee cavaliere au bois de Boulogne (Bridle-alley in the Bois de Boulogne)* (1873), in the exhibition Renoir – between Bohemian and Bourgoisie: the early years, at the museum of Fine Arts in Basel, Switzerland.

the admiration of the emerging modernist avant-garde and is still, today, regarded as one of the most creative geniuses the art world has ever seen.

The largest collection of Renoir's works is not housed in France, but at the Barnes Foundation, near Philadelphia, Pennsylvania in the United States. The foundation is home to 181 paintings.

Books

History and Techniques of the Great Masters: Renoir (A Quarto Book) by Guy Jennings (August 1988)

Pierre-Auguste Renoir, Mon Pere (Folio) by Jean Renoir (January 20, 1988)

Renoir by Anne Distel (February 25, 2010)

Renoir by Auguste Renoir (1985)

Renoir (Phaidon Colour Library) by William Gaunt (July 1992)

Renoir: His Life and Works in 500 Images: An Illustrated Exploration of the Artist, His Life and Context by Susie Hodge (September 12, 2011)

Renoir, My Father (NYRB Classics) by Jean Renoir and Robert L. Herbert (September 1, 2001)

Renoir on Renoir: Interviews, Essays, and Remarks (Cambridge Studies in Film) by Jean Renoir and Carol Volk (March 30, 1990)

Renoir's Garden by Jacques Renoir and Derek Fell (March 9, 1995)

Rockwell Heist: The Extraordinary Theft of Seven Norman Rockwell Painting & a Phony Renoir... by Bruce Rubenstein (March 1, 2013)

(PA Photos)

■ **ABOVE:** **Exhibition Renoir/Renoir held in the new Cinematheque Francaise in Paris, shows parallels between the works of Renoir and his son, movie director Jean Renoir.**